Thank you to my family for encouraging me to do a second book!

Jeremiah 29:11
"For I know the plans I have for you," declares the Lord, "plans to prosper you and not to harm you, plans to give you hope and a future."

Beverly Orange

Spring had finally arrived, and Beechy the Bear could hardly contain his excitement as he dashed through the meadow, eager to find his friends.

He wondered what they had been doing all winter while he was hibernating. Surely, they had been playing in the meadow, especially on such a beautiful day. The sun beamed down on the bright, bushy trees, their branches now heavy with fresh, green leaves.

As he was heading to the meadow, he couldn't believe all the different flowers he spotted: daisies, daffodils, lilies, and bluebells. There were so many!

At the edge of the forest, he ran into Wayne the Wolf.
"Hey, Beechy! What's the rush?" Wayne called out.

"I'm looking for my friends! I can't wait to play with them,"
Beechy replied enthusiastically.
"Can I join you?" Wayne asked, his tail wagging. "I heard
there's an Easter egg hunt today!"
"That would be great," Beechy grinned. "I've never played
before, but it sounds fun!"
"Me neither!" Wayne said. "I wonder what it's all about?"

"Wow! I can't believe what I'm seeing!" Beechy exclaimed, scooping up a brightly colored egg.

Just then, he spotted Blake the Badger and Taylor the Turtle holding a basket. "Hey, guys! What are you up to?" Beechy asked. "We're on an Easter egg hunt!" Taylor replied with a big grin.

"An Easter egg hunt?" Beechy tilted his head. "Wayne said you were playing, but neither of us knows what it is. What are the rules?"

Blake chuckled. "We have one every year for Easter!"
"Easter?" Beechy looked puzzled. "What's that?"

Before anyone could answer, Rucker the Rabbit and Sammy the Squirrel hopped over, their baskets brimming with eggs. "Hey, everyone! I found seven eggs! How many have you all found?" Rucker asked excitedly.

"I've found one," Beechy replied, "but I still don't know what Easter is!"

Carrie the Cardinal swooped in from above and landed gracefully beside them. "How's the Easter egg hunt going?" Hi, Beechy! It's so nice to see you!"

"Hey, Carrie!" Beechy smiled. "I was just about to learn about Easter. Do you know why we have Easter eggs?"

Carrie nodded. "I do! Easter eggs have a special story. Hold on—I'll get James. He loves Easter egg hunts and can tell you all about it."

A moment later, James the Jay Bird landed beside them.

"A long time ago, eggs were a symbol of new life and rebirth. Early Christians dyed eggs in different colors to tell parts of the Easter story—white for purity, blue for baptism, green for growing in faith, red for the blood Jesus shed, dark colors for the sadness in the world, and gold to remind us of Heaven."

Rucker chimed in, "But that's just part of it. The real story of Easter is even bigger!"

Beechy's eyes widened. "Really? What else is there?"

Rucker took a deep breath. "Let me tell you about Jesus. He's the whole reason for Easter."

Beechy leaned in, listening closely as Rucker began to share the story of Easter—a story of love, hope, and new beginnings. "Easter is all about Jesus. He is our Lord and Savior," Rucker explained.
Beechy listened carefully. "What does that mean?"

"Well," Rucker continued, "a long time ago, Jesus came to show us love and kindness. But He also did something very special for us. He died, was buried, and then—on the third day—He rose from the grave! Now, He is alive and with us today."

Beechy's eyes grew wide. "So, Easter is really about celebrating Jesus coming back to life?"
"Exactly!" Carrie said with a smile. "The eggs and the hunt remind us of the new life and hope Jesus gives us."

Beechy looked at his colorful eggs. "Wow. I had no idea Easter was so important. Thanks for sharing that story, Rucker." "Anytime," Rucker replied warmly. "Easter reminds us that love, hope, and new beginnings are always with us because of Jesus."

As their baskets began to overflow with eggs, they made their way to Debbie the Deer, where she and Ogden the Owl were waiting with prizes for the Easter egg hunt.

Carrie and James hovered above, holding an Easter banner, while Eric the Eagle perched nearby, watched the festivities.

"Who found the most eggs?" Debbie asked excitedly.
Blake stepped forward proudly. "I found twenty-five eggs!"

"Wow, Blake! You won the grand prize!" Debbie cheered, handing him a beautifully wrapped gift.
Ogden grinned. "Now, who found the golden egg?"

Taylor stepped forward, holding the shiny golden egg high. "I did!"
"Well done, Taylor! For finding the golden egg, you get a special
prize too," Ogden said, handing Taylor a shimmering blue ribbon
and a bag of goodies.

Happy Easter

Beechy beamed as he looked around at his friends, realizing that Easter was about more than eggs and prizes. It was about celebrating love, hope, and the joy of being together.

As the friends admired their prizes and colorful eggs, Eric the Eagle landed nearby, his wings outstretched as he greeted everyone.

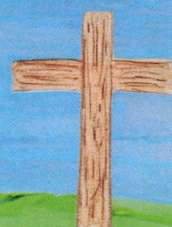

"Hey, Eric!" Wayne waved.
Eric looked around at his friends with a warm smile. "Hi, Wayne."

"This has been so much fun," he said, "but let's remember that the true meaning of Easter is that Jesus is alive and with us today. Easter is a celebration of His love and the hope He brings."

The friends nodded thoughtfully, each feeling a little closer and warmer, knowing Easter was about more than eggs and prizes. It was about love, hope, and the joy of knowing Jesus is always with them.

Beechy smiled, his heart full of joy. "Thank you, Eric. I'll never forget that."

For God so loved the world, that he gave his only begotten Son, that whosoever believeth in him should not perish, but have everlasting life. John 3:16

Thank you again to my friend Amanda Waldron for editing my book.

If you enjoyed this book, please check out my first book. Beechy Bear Discovers Christmas.

Made in the USA
Middletown, DE
16 February 2025